MEXICAN FOREIGN POLICY
AT THE TURN OF THE CENTURY:
HOW DOMESTIC A FOREIGN POLICY?

Ana Covarrubias

The Institute for the Study of the Americas publishes in its Lecture Series selected seminar and conference papers and public lectures delivered at the Institute by scholars associated with the work of the Institute.

This work is an overview of the research project 'Mexico's Changing Place in the World', which is based at Oxford University's Centre for Mexican Studies. I am grateful to my colleagues at the Centre and at the Institute of Latin American Studies (now the Institute for the Study of the Americas) for their comments on preliminary versions of this paper.

First published 2005 by
Institute for the Study of the Americas
31 Tavistock Square
London
WC1H 9HA

Copyright © 2005 Institute for the Study of the Americas

All rights reserved. No part of this book may be reproduced, stored in a retrieval system, or transmitted, in any form, or by any means, electronic, mechanical, photocopying, recording or otherwise without the prior written permission of the publishers.

British Library Cataloguing-in-Publication Data
A British Library CIP record is available.

ISBN 1-900039-65-6

Typeset in Bembo by
Koinonia, Bury, Lancashire

Contents

I	Sources and nature of foreign policy	*page* 5
II	The idea of a 'traditional' foreign policy	9
III	New paths or new styles of walking?	17
IV	New and active foreign policies: ruptures and alternancias	34
V	Reflections on change: how new is new, how active is active, and how different can it get?	41

1 Sources and nature of foreign policy

The process that culminated in the signature of the North American Free Trade Agreement, NAFTA, prompted a discussion about the 'new orientation' of Mexico's foreign policy. A foreign policy that moved away from 'traditional' standings was strongly criticised by many, but this was obviously not the first time that change in foreign policy was considered. On this occasion, however, the discussion was part of a broader debate about major transformations in the international system, especially as a result of the end of the Cold War, and also regarding changes within Mexico. The official discourse of many countries, a number of academic works and the media highlighted change as a positive development in international history: a new world order was, after all, President George Bush's stated aim. Consequently, scholars faced the challenge of assessing the form and implication of new international trends; analysts of Mexican politics, in turn, had to identify the causality and the links between changes at different levels: the international system, domestic politics and economics, and foreign policy.

The task of understanding the new direction of foreign policy was facilitated by the election of Vicente Fox in 2002, when the official discourse decidedly adopted the idea of a *new* foreign policy, defined as *active*, and gave it a predominant place in the government's priorities. The foreign policy project identified 'strategic' objectives, such as the promotion of democracy and the protection of human rights at the international level, and the development of a long-term view of a North American region; the direction of change seemed clear.[1] The characterisation of Mexico's *new* foreign policy would require a review of Mexico's foreign policy in the past, and of the ways in which it was analysed. Such an exercise surpasses the scope of this work, but it will hopefully make a contribution along that path, by looking at three issues that have

---

[1] Mexico, Secretaría de Relaciones Exteriores, 'Visión, Misión y Objetivos de la Secretaría de Relaciones Exteriores' <http://www.sre.gob.mx>, accessed 29 January 2004.

encouraged the discussion about change over the last twenty years: economic foreign relations, US–Mexico relations and the meaning of 'domestic issues'.[2]

This paper will focus on two main components of foreign policy – sources and nature – taking as a starting point those questions formulated by James Rosenau and Peter Gourevitch in two well-known works on foreign policy analysis: 'to what extent and under what circumstances is each source, domestic and international, more or less causal than the others?' and 'which aspect of domestic structure (or international for that matter) best explains how a country behaves in the international sphere?'[3] This approach to foreign policy analysis is certainly not new, but these simple questions may still be helpful in qualifying views that give either globalisation or Mexico's domestic transformations almost full explanatory power as to the country's external behaviour, by reminding us of a variety of factors that influence, and on occasions determine, foreign policy. The ultimate objective of this type of analysis would be to trace such influence and to explain how and why different factors are operative under certain circumstances and not others.[4] This paper intends to identify those factors and suggest ways in which they influenced Mexican foreign policy over the last twenty years, but only as a first approximation, leaving for future research a systematic comparison of issues and periods that would allow us to establish regular patterns.

There is a vast literature on foreign policy analysis that looks at sources, from decision-making and national culture, on the domestic front or *the inside*, to political economy and the distribution of power at the international level or *the outside*. This work will consider regime type and the economic model as the main domestic variables, and the international

---

2   These are not, of course, the only issues that can illustrate change and continuity in Mexican foreign policy; the environment, for example, is another pertinent topic. Given the impossibility of covering all issues in Mexican foreign policy, I will limit the analysis to these three, as representative cases.

3   James Roseanau, 'Pre-theories and Theories of Foreign Policy,' in R. Barry Farrell (ed.), *Approaches to Comparative and International Politics* (Evanston: Northwestern University Press, 1966), p. 41, and Peter Gourevitch, 'The Second Image Reversed: The International Sources of Domestic Politics,' *International Organization*, vol. 32, no. 4, autumn 1978, p. 900.

4   Rosenau, 'Pre-theories and Theories of Foreign Policy,' p. 31.

economy – globalisation – and the distribution of power – unipolarity – as the most relevant international variables.[5]

This paper will argue that the transformations that gave rise to claims about *the* change in Mexican foreign policy were primarily economic and started in the early 1980s. Such transformations were consolidated relatively quickly and resulted in an open economy and the adoption of free trade. A new attitude on issues of a more political nature, however, began to take shape towards the mid-1990s, and the process has continued to this day in a cautious and gradual way. Throughout these years, Mexican governments have come to see what for many years were considered 'domestic issues' – democracy and human rights – in a different light, accepting them in fact as 'intermestic issues'. Political and economic transformations were linked, in one way or another, to the United States so that bilateral relations *per se* were also a cause and a consequence of change in foreign policy.

Interestingly, the reshaping of foreign policy was related to domestic circumstances, such as economic crises, a closed political regime and violations of human rights, not to external events, but international factors did act as catalysts. In other words, foreign policy changed because of domestic problems, but the problems were pointed out by external actors, who had a notable interest in them. In other words, *the outside* was determinant, firstly, because it provided the hierarchy of 'important issues' to address in both international and domestic politics: economic neo-liberalism, democracy and human rights. Secondly, *the outside* was influential to the extent that it was either 'the alternative', as in the case of the opening of the Mexican economy and NAFTA, or the audience: Presidents Carlos Salinas (1988–1994), Ernesto Zedillo (1994–2000) and Vicente Fox (2000–) all wanted to project a certain image of Mexico abroad. *The inside* is obviously indispensable as the home of the foreign policy making process: throughout history, presidents have had a fundamental role in foreign policy, but Congress and public opinion have also been gaining in influence: if not decisive, they are at least significant in creating a different

5 Regime type refers to not only the formal legal and institutional arrangements, but also the politics behind them. For a recent discussion on sources of foreign policy see Christopher Hill, *The Changing Politics of Foreign Policy* (London: Palgrave MacMillan, 2003), pp. 219–49.

context in which to design and implement foreign policy. *The inside* was, however, also crucial insofar as it became the target of foreign policy; that is, foreign policy became an instrument of domestic politics. The NAFTA and President Fox's foreign policy were – and *is* in the case of Fox – two strategies intended to lock-in domestic reform: economic liberalisation and democratic change. In the latter case, *the inside* also becomes relevant as the current government tries to portray foreign policy as the continuation of domestic politics i.e., the projection of Mexico's new democratic values. To summarise, starting from internal circumstances, the international variable was decisive, but the adoption of changes in foreign policy had a domestic timing. After all, the Mexican government could have opened up the country's economy and political process during the 1980s, but it took longer than this (except for economic liberalisation, which started abruptly in the mid-1980s). This delayed reaction, to the demands, requests or expectations of the international agenda may be explained by domestic processes.

The paper will start by looking briefly at Mexico's so-called 'traditional' foreign policy to establish the terms of the discussion regarding both the sources for, and the nature of, foreign policy. It will then turn to identify changes in economic foreign policy, in the relations with the United States and in the understanding of 'domestic issues' and, with the purpose of enriching the analysis and expanding on President Fox's foreign policy, a further section will compare the latter with that of President Luis Echeverría (1970–1976). The final conclusions of this work will provide a broader picture of Mexico's foreign policy over the last twenty years and a better understanding of where it stands today.

II The idea of a 'traditional' foreign policy

Although any foreign policy is, by definition,[6] not constant and may be highly reactive (more so for relatively weak countries), it is still possible to identify certain continuities in the form of general trends: recurrent positions with regard to certain issues in international politics and, in the Mexican case at least, an official rhetoric that was so constant and well defined, it actually became a useful diplomatic tool. Analytically, such trends or orientations are useful as a point of reference with which to assess change, despite the existence of significant exceptions.

Mexican foreign policy after the Second World War has been studied mostly in chronological order, either according to *sexenios*, or in longer segments: before the 1970s, the 1970s and early 1980s, the 1980s and the 1990s. In 1956, a prestigious Mexican diplomat, Jorge Castañeda, characterised Mexico's foreign policy as 'a barrier; a defence to protect internal development against certain external factors'.[7] Mexico, according to Castañeda, had no direct political, territorial, strategic or economic interests beyond its borders, and it did not exert hegemony or have interests to protect in areas of international conflict. Additionally, Mexico was not attentive to international affairs because of an accentuated nationalism and

---

6 At the beginning of his book, Christopher Hill states an initial definition of foreign policy: 'the sum of official external relations conducted by an independent actor (usually a state) in international relations'. He, of course, acknowledges various problems with this definition (such as who can be counted as 'foreign policy-makers') but it is still useful for the purposes of this work because it points to other implicit elements such as politics (the notion of *policy*) and coherence that make foreign policy different from 'external relations'. Hence the definition of foreign policy as: '... attempts to coordinate, and it is the way in which – at least in principle – priorities are established between competing externally-projected interests. It should also project the values which the society in question thinks are universal ...' Hill, *The Changing Politics,* pp. 3–5.
7 Jorge Castañeda, 'México y el orden internacional,' *Obras Completas* (vol. I *Naciones Unidas*) (Mexico: Instituto Matías Romero de Estudios Diplomáticos, SRE-El Colegio de México, 1995), p. 45.

due to an understanding of international relations as purely bilateral. Castañeda, however, underlined the fact that the time might have come to develop a foreign policy which would foster a positive role with regards to the concerns of 'smaller' countries: the maintenance of international peace, the preservation of independence, the predominance of international Law and the acceleration of social and economic development.[8]

In effect, until the 1970s Mexican foreign policy is usually characterised as *passive*:[9] Mexican governments were mainly concerned with domestic political stability and economic development, having no significant 'global interests' i.e., no interests abroad. Mario Ojeda and Olga Pellicer argue that Mexican governments were reluctant to get involved in international 'high politics' and preferred isolation, but such a view is perhaps more accurately understood in terms of the ways in which Mexican governments acted, as, after all, isolation was not possible and, on occasions, Mexican governments both reacted to and adopted a more positive attitude towards international events. A few examples may suffice to demonstrate Mexico's presence in the international sphere. Firstly, Mexican governments demonstrated a strong interest in the design of the post-war international system, both regarding the United Nations and the Organization of American States (OAS), Mexico was therefore not entirely indifferent as to how the international system would work, and should work.[10] Secondly, in a rigidly bipolar world, Mexican governments established relations with socialist countries and participated as observer in the Non-Aligned Movement. It is true that these actions may not, strictly speaking, be foreign policy, and that they may be rather insignificant, but they still indicate a certain involvement in world politics, and more

8 *Ibid.*, pp. 39–49.
9 This definition is a simplification of what Mario Ojeda originally called an attitude as opposed to a policy, which implied action and initiative. Mexico, according to Ojeda, had a passive international attitude that was mostly defensive, that openly sought isolationism and which was based on principles of a negative nature. However, since Ojeda also considers these defining elements of a passive attitude a 'tactic' of foreign policy, I will refer to a passive foreign policy. Mario Ojeda, *Alcances y límites de la política exterior de México* (Mexico: El Colegio de México, 1976), pp. 100–6.
10 Mexico's participation at the Inter-American Conference on the Problems of War and Pace (the Chapultepec Conference, 1945) and its views on the Dumbarton Oaks proposals for the creation of the United Nations are good examples.

importantly, they suggest Mexico's room for manoeuvre in a difficult and highly ideological international environment. Lastly, Mexican governments reacted to regional events such as the 1954 Guatemalan coup, the Cuban Revolution, the Cuban Missile Crisis and the invasion of the Dominican Republic, in ways not always comfortable to, or welcomed by, OAS members, especially the United States.[11] Whatever its reasons or motivations, Mexico was visible in the inter-American system. True, Mexico's was not always a 'political' policy in the sense that it did not discuss the political issue at stake and its emphasis was mainly juridical (frequently concerned more with matters of procedure).[12] Mexico's international presence was significant enough, however, to consolidate a clear image of a consistent and well-defined foreign policy.

Explanations of this *passive* foreign policy, that was not inactive, vary. As the international system is concerned, the United States is obviously a key variable, explaining Mexico's foreign policy through three interrelated propositions: a) the so called dilemma of Mexico's foreign policy: to defend non-intervention whilst at the same time not opposing the United States too much; b) the existence of an 'agreement to disagree' between the United States and Mexico: Mexico disagrees with the United States on issues of great importance to Mexico but not to the United States, and Mexico cooperates with regard to issues critical to the United States that have little relevance for Mexico; c) US interest in Mexico's internal stability. Beyond the United States, one might also point at an external environment that is generally indifferent to Mexican internal politics.[13]

Within Mexico, Jorge Chabat identifies two major variables: 'a closed economic model that inhibited contacts with the outside', and 'a closed political model that built a façade of internal unanimity and fed a

---

[11] This view is beginning to change as more documents that prove that in the end Mexican governments agreed with the United States are being declassified. See US, Department of State, *Foreign Relations of the United States, 1958–1960. American Republics* (vol. 5, 1991).

[12] Ojeda, *Alcances y límites*, p. 101.

[13] *Ibid.* pp. 80, 93 ; Jorge Chabat, 'Mexican Foreign Policy in the 1990s: Learning to Live with Interdependence,' in Heraldo Muñoz and Joseph Tulchin (eds), *Latin American Nations in World Politics*, 2nd ed. (Boulder: Westview Press, 1996), p. 152.

vociferous nationalism'.[14] The permanence of the PRI in power and the role of the president in the political regime have also accounted for the nature of foreign policy; a policy that was not very much influenced by discussions in Congress or interest groups, for example, and that was only exceptionally of great interest to public opinion.[15] The features of the Mexican political regime surely contributed to shaping an official discourse, which, in turn, nourished the image of a constant, predictable and coherent foreign policy. As already mentioned, no matter how political the issue in question was, or how political their own interests were, Mexican governments usually resorted to legalistic arguments implicit in a 'policy of principles'. Although speaking in the 1980s, the words of former Secretary of Foreign Affairs, Bernardo Sepúlveda, neatly summarise the government's own understanding of Mexico's foreign policy 'of principles':

> By conviction and necessity, throughout its post-revolutionary history, Mexico has endorsed a body of principles that has conducted its foreign policy at all times. It is not however a policy that leans on abstract notions. The reality is that those principles respond in an integral way to the nation's most legitimate interests. When Mexico defends non-intervention, self-determination, peaceful resolution of disputes, juridical equality of states and cooperation for development, it defends something more than just theoretical postulates; it defends its right to be a sovereign people before the rest of the peoples. They are, on the other hand, principles which violation Mexico has been the victim of throughout its history and which universal validity and compliance would constitute a pillar to defend the country.[16]

14 Chabat, 'Mexican Foreign Policy in the 1990s,' p. 152. Features of an authoritarian regime may be a relevant variable here, despite formal democracy, division of powers and federalism.
15 Ojeda argues that it was not only the fact that the same party stayed in power for so long, but also that it never faced a well-organised and important opposition. Ojeda, *Alcances y límites*, p. 96. Cuba may be an illustrative exception, since the 1959 Revolution did have an impact on Mexican society, and groups for and against Castro's government and Mexico's policy towards it clashed, physically even. See Olga Pellicer, *México y la revolución cubana* (Mexico: El Colegio de México, 1976).
16 Bernardo Sepúlveda Amor, 'Reflexiones sobre la política exterior de México,' *Foro Internacional*, vol. 24, no. 4, April-June 1984, p. 409. Interestingly, the quote implicitly looks at the external sphere to explain Mexico's foreign policy. The international

Ojeda agrees that the principles of non-intervention and the right to self-determination became a cornerstone of Mexico's foreign policy as a consequence of the country's history, and argues that they became a shield behind which Mexico could survive as a sovereign state. Non-intervention was, however, also a means to keep the country away from problems in the world. Mexico's 'international attitude' changed, however, as the 1970s progressed.[17]

The 1970s and early 1980s are known as the period with an *active* foreign policy as the Mexican government pursued its own initiatives and, on occasions, backed them substantially with material resources and strong diplomatic positions. The shift to an *active* foreign policy implied that it was *new*. Mexico became visible in the international system broadly speaking, and not only in the regional sub-system. President Luis Echeverría's *active* foreign policy will be discussed in greater detail below, and included his proposal for a New Economic International Order, NIEO, the country's rapprochement with Salvador Allende's Chile and Cuba, and its distance from Francisco Franco's Spain. In turn, President José López Portillo's government (1976–1982) implemented an unusually dynamic policy towards Central America, which suggested that Mexico had attained the status of middle power. Mexico's material support to the Sandinista government, and to a lesser extent the Salvadoran guerrilla, has been well documented.[18]

---

system, or Mexico's position in the world, very much defines the nature of the country's foreign policy; a foreign policy that became *the* foreign policy of Mexican – PRI – governments. This is a mostly rhetorical position, as foreign policy was not immutable over the years of PRI rule, nor did it always follow strict principles, but it is still valuable for what it reflects about the way in which Mexican governments understood and managed foreign policy, at least publicly. Foreign policy was defined *outside-in* rather than *inside-out*. Hill would explain such a statement, and policy, on the basis of domestic culture: 'traumas encountered in world politics, but once certain social attitudes and political forces are established they feed back to affect the future foreign policy choices, often with serious consequences'. Hill, *The Changing Politics,* p. 227.

17 Ojeda, *Alcances y límites,* p. 101.
18 Gabriel Rosenzweig, 'La cooperación económica de México con Centroamérica a partir de 1979: Perspectivas para los próximos años,' in Olga Pellicer (ed.), *La política exterior de México: desafíos en los ochenta* (Mexico: CIDE, 1983), pp. 235–72; Mario Ojeda and René Herrera, *La política de México hacia Centroamérica, 1979–1982* (Mexico: El Colegio de México, 1983) (Jornadas, 103); Jorge G. Castañeda, '¿Qué hacemos en Centroamérica?, *México: El futuro en juego* (Mexico: Joaquín Mortiz-Planeta, 1987).

López Portillo tried to mediate between Nicaragua and its neighbours, proposed a Peace Plan for Central America, improved relations with Cuba to their best state ever, and together with France issued a Declaration recognising the Salvadoran guerrilla movement as a legitimate political force. Additionally, Mexico hosted the North-South Meeting in Cancún in an attempt to present the country as a 'mediator' between those two blocs.

The best known study of Echeverría's foreign policy underlines the influence of domestic concerns,[19] as will be seen below, but it should also be mentioned that Echeverría's foreign policy took place in a more flexible international system, the *détente* and, perhaps, through what Abraham Lowenthal called the 'declining' hegemony of the United States.[20] In brief, such a system opened spaces for Mexican action. In the case of Central America, even as *détente* faded, the situation in the region gave Mexico the opportunity to act; whether the Mexican government had necessarily to react to it, or whether it was one among other policy options is still a matter for discussion. A more realistic interpretation would look at Mexico's increase in domestic capabilities as a result of oil wealth: a more powerful country could project a more decisive foreign policy. On the political side, and considering Echeverría as well, two considerations are worth underlining: firstly, the primacy of leaders and, secondly, the self-claimed 'revolutionary/progressive' nature of the regime. There is little doubt that a Third World Policy and Central America are easily identified as Echeverría and López Portillo's foreign policy; and, in both cases, the two presidents resorted to Mexico's progressive and revolutionary legacy to make sense of their policies towards Chile, Cuba, Nicaragua and El Salvador. Such a rhetoric certainly facilitated relations with those countries, or with the guerrilla in the Salvadorean case.[21] It should be said, however,

---

19 Yoram Shapira, *Mexican Foreign Policy under Echeverría* (London: Sage, 1978), or, in Spanish, 'La política exterior de México bajo el régimen de Echeverría,' *Foro Internacional*, vol. 19, no. 1(73), July-September 1978, pp. 62–91.

20 Abraham Lowenthal, 'The United States and Latin America: ending the hegemonic presumption,' *Foreign Affairs*, 55, October 1976, pp. 199–213. Whether US hegemony was declining or not may be the subject for discussion but what is more difficult to deny is that the US government's attention was not predominantly in Latin America, but in other areas, such as Vietnam, and in other issues, such as the international economy.

21 See for example López Portillo's address to the Sandinistas in 1981. José López Portillo, *Mis tiempos. Biografía y testimonio político* (Mexico: Fernández Editores, 1988), pp. 925–26.

that on these occasions Mexico's policy was criticised inside Mexico: different groups questioned the government's support of Chilean exiles, including members of the Allende family, Fidel Castro, the Sandinistas and the Salvadorean guerrillas, but there is still no evidence that these voices of dissent actually had any influence in shaping or redirecting foreign policy. Moreover, as Mexico searched for a leading role in international and regional politics, the usefulness, but more importantly, the observance of foreign policy 'principles' was increasingly questioned. Interestingly however, Mexico not only continued to have an active participation in Central America in the 1980s, but principles were incorporated into the Mexican Constitution towards the end of de la Madrid's government (1982–1988). Section X of Article 89 specifies that, in conducting foreign policy, 'the Executive Power will observe the following ruling principles: self-determination; non-intervention; peaceful resolution of disputes; the proscription of the threat or the use of force in international relations; juridical equality of states; international cooperation for development; and the fight for international peace and security'.[22] The official discourse prevailed despite a more erratic foreign policy.

Mexico's participation in the Contadora Group (1983) has also been explained mostly in terms of international considerations: officially, unrest in Central America posed a national security risk, especially as the number of Guatemalan refugees in Mexican territory increased; analysts, on the other hand, argued that Mexico's policy was intended to avoid a direct US military intervention in the region as it would only aggravate the already delicate situation leading, perhaps, to a general war in the isthmus.[23] Once

---

22 *Constitución Política de los Estados Unidos Mexicanos* <http://www.segob.mx>, accessed 19 March 2004.
23 René Herrera and Manuel Chavarría, 'México en Contadora: una búsqueda de límites a su compromiso en Centroamérica,' *Foro Internacional*, vol. 24, no. 4(96), April-June 1984, pp. 458–483; Olga Pellicer, 'México en Centroamérica: el difícil ejercicio del poder regional,' in Olga Pellicer and Richard Fagen (eds.), *Centroamérica: futuro y opciones* (Mexico: FCE, 1983), pp. 97–112; Mario Ojeda, *México: El surgimiento de una política exterior activa* (Mexico: SEP, 1986); Tom J. Farer, 'Contadora: The Hidden Agenda,' *Foreign Policy*, no. 59, summer, 1985, p. 59; Miguel de la Madrid, 'Los nuevos retos de México,' in UNAM, *México en Centroamérica. Expediente de Documentos Fundamentales 1979–1986* (Mexico: Centro de Investigaciones Interdisciplinarias en Humanidades, 1989), p. 80.

again, Mexico's actions were understood by both officials and academics as a means of projecting an autonomous foreign policy; that is, different from that of the United States. According to Lorenzo Meyer, Mexico's policy in Central America was a means to facilitate the survival of Mexican nationalism.[24]

The United States, in effect, was a key reference to Mexico's foreign policy during the presidency of Miguel de la Madrid. Its influence, however, was projected in two divergent ways: on the economic front, differences between the two governments diminished significantly;[25] political disagreement, on the other hand, was profound. In this sense, the 'agreement to disagree' seems to have worked, but only just. The question again is why did Mexico decide to act in Contadora in an adverse international system? Was it really necessary?

---

24 Josefina Zoraida Vázquez and Lorenzo Meyer, *México frente a Estados Unidos. Un ensayo histórico, 1776–1980* (Mexico: El Colegio de México, 1982), pp. 211–26.
25 For a discussion on how the Mexican and US governments differed in terms of its economics and trade, see María Celia Toro, 'El comercio México-Estados Unidos: la realidad desigual y los límites a la colaboración norteamericana,' in Pellicer (ed.), *La política exterior de México*, ,pp. 187–234.

III New paths or new styles of walking?

Although the emphasis on the novelty of the world emerging in the 1990s has been rightly questioned, the passage from the Cold War to globalisation implied transformations of certain international conditions that had consequences inside the countries and between them. Guadalupe González has identified three major changes at the end of the Cold War that affected countries like Mexico (intermediate countries): 1. the presence of a less predictable superpower whose foreign policy agenda was influenced more decisively by domestic political factors; 2. an uncertain international leadership that invited intermediate countries to act; and, 3. the disjunction of military and economic power at the global level that increased the importance of regional relations and resulted in the emergence of a more regionally differentiated world.[26] Accordingly, changes in Mexican foreign policy were the result of an uneven adjustment to globalisation in three stages: unilateral opening for diversification (1985–1990); active bilateralism (1990–1994), and partial retreat (1994–1999). Throughout these stages, 'Mexico gradually moved from an ideologically driven and politically centred nationalist diplomacy to a more economically focused and segmented pragmatic foreign policy.'[27] González's framework is an excellent starting point to look at three specific foreign policy topics, hoping to find the extent of change and continuity, and the links between domestic and international variables. The contrast between the 'partial retreat' stage proposed by González with President Fox's initial *active* foreign policy and an ensuing 'partial retreat' may also enrich the discussion.

---

26 Guadalupe González, 'Foreign Policy Strategies in a Globalized World: the Case of Mexico,' in Joseph S. Tulchin and Ralph H. Espach (eds.), *Latin America in the New International System* (Boulder: Lynne Rienner, 2001), p. 144.
27 *Ibid.* p. 152.

The economy and foreign relations

Mexican foreign policy was obviously affected by the shift in economic model initiated by Miguel de la Madrid's government. As a response to the situation of the economy during and after the debt crisis, the Mexican government made a series of reforms in the direction of a liberal, market oriented economy, along the lines set by the IMF and the World Bank. The Mexican government's decision to join the GATT in 1986 is usually taken as the best illustration of the country's new economic direction. This was the beginning, according to González, of a new outward-oriented grand strategy; a strategy, however, that had to develop under adverse circumstances in the country, namely a profound economic vulnerability and political instability, and as strategic options outside the Western Hemisphere narrowed down.[28]

NAFTA represented the consolidation or the open acknowledgement of change in the economic model, and the process towards its conclusion also indicated the ways in which Mexico was willing to relate to the world, and how it wanted to be perceived by foreign actors. Mexico's reasons for joining NAFTA are well known: to reactivate the economy and to lock-in domestic reforms. Foreign investment and trade with secure external markets were badly needed, and neither Europe nor Japan was a viable option. A treaty with the United States, therefore, would establish rules and procedures to put in order an ongoing process of economic integration between the two countries.[29] The Bush administration, on its part, thought that NAFTA would serve to accelerate a wider free trade liberalisation process, especially as progress in the Uruguay Round was very slow. Moreover, NAFTA, as a Mexican initiative, would assist the United States in redefining a troublesome relationship with its southern neighbour. From both the economic and the political perspectives, in

---

28 Ibid., p.151.
29 Gustavo Del Castillo and Gustavo Vega, 'The North American Free Trade Agreement in context. A Mexican Perspective,' in Gustavo del Castillo and Gustavo Vega (eds.), *The Politics of Free Trade in North America* (Ottawa: Center for Trade Policy and Law, 1995), pp. 83–151.; González, 'Foreign Policy Strategies,'; Jorge I. Domínguez and Rafael Fernández de Castro, *The United States and Mexico: Between Partnership and Conflict* (New York: Routledge, 2001), pp. 24–34.

brief, NAFTA could advance Bush's idea of a new world order. Finally, the conclusion of NAFTA was facilitated by an international system that stressed the ideas of co-operation and institutions, and by the nature of leadership in both countries.[30] NAFTA however was not a perfect picture, and it could not escape the politics of economic integration: two parallel accords were necessary, so as not to include environment and labour issues in the main treaty, and Mexican oil was protected from foreign investment.

NAFTA then can be seen as the cause and consequence of a very dynamic commercial policy, González's active bilateralism, which gave foreign policy a clear economic content and provided it with tools not used before, such as lobbying in the US Congress or approaching the Mexican community living in the United States.[31] Equally important was the number of actors that participated actively in the foreign policy making process (Bank of Mexico, the Ministries of Finance and of Industrial Promotion and Foreign Trade, certain businessmen groups), or that tried to influence it in various directions, (NGOs in the areas of environment, labour or human rights, medium and small businessmen's groups, etc).[32] During the 1980s and 1990s, Mexico embraced a view of economic development that brought the world into the Mexican economy and took Mexico's economy to the world, and such a view certainly contrasted with previous development strategies. This process would inevitably have consequences in domestic and foreign policy: by the time NAFTA was

30 Jorge I. Domínguez, 'Mexico's New Foreign Policy: States, Societies, and Institutions,' in Rodolfo O. de la Garza and Jesús Velasco (eds.), *Bridging the Border. Transforming Mexico-US Relations* (Lanham: Rowman and Littlefield, 1997), p. 193; Domínguez and Fernández de Castro, *The United States and Mexico*, p. 25.
31 See Todd Eisenstadt, 'The Rise of the Mexico Lobby in Washington: Even Further from God, and Even Closer to the United States'; Jorge Chabat, 'Mexico's Foreign Policy after NAFTA: The Tools of Interdependence'; and Carlos González Gutiérrez, 'Decentralized Diplomacy: The Role of Consular Offices in Mexico's Relations with its Diaspora,' in De la Garza and Velasco, (eds.), *Bridging the Border,* pp. 89–124, 33–47 and 49–67 respectively.
32 Domínguez and Fernández de Castro, *The United States and Mexico*; González, 'Foreign Policy Strategies,' and for other topics, such as the environment, see Blanca Torres, 'La participación de actores nuevos y tradicionales en las relaciones internacionales de México,' in Centro de Estudios Internacionales-Instituto Matías Romero de Estudios Diplomáticos, *La política exterior de México: Enfoques para su análisis* (Mexico, 1997), pp. 119–5.

signed, Mexico had incorporated the issues of free trade and economic liberalisation that ranked at the top of the international agenda in its own foreign policy. For the first time in the twentieth Century, according to González, market forces and political choices reinforced each other in expanding Mexico's integration into the world economy: between 1980 and 1998, the share of exports to GDP almost tripled from 11 to 31.9 per cent, increasing the degree of exposure of the Mexican economy to international markets and the decisions of foreign governmental and nongovernmental actors. In 1998, total foreign trade represented 64.3 per cent of Mexico's GDP.[33] In a period of ten years Mexico became a member of APEC (1993) and the OECD (1994), and signed around 10 free trade agreements with countries in Latin America, Europe and the Middle East.[34]

Mexico–USA relations

The United States has 'no more important relationship in the world than the one we have with Mexico' said President George W. Bush during Fox's visit to the United States in September 2001.[35] Until then, both presidents had proclaimed the beginning of a new era in Mexico–US relations, including a 'Partnership for Prosperity'.[36] Such an era, however,

33 González, 'Foreign Policy Strategies,' p. 141. Data from the World Bank indicate that trade in goods as a share of GDP was 54.2 per cent in 2001; in turn, foreign direct investment (net flows in reporting country, current USD) increased from 11.9 billion USD to 24.7 billion in 2001. Exports of goods and services as share of GDP were 27.3 per cent in 2001, imports decreased from 32.8 per cent to 29.7 per cent in 1998 and 2001. The World Bank, 'Mexico Data Profile,' <http://devdata.worldbank.org/external/CPProfile.asp?SelectedCountry=MEX&CCOD...>, accessed 23 February 2004.
34 Chile (1992); NAFTA, (1994); Group of Three [Colombia and Venezuela], Bolivia and Costa Rica (1995); Nicaragua (1998); EU and Israel (2000); EFTA, Uruguay [Economic Complementary Treaty] and the Northern Triangle [Guatemala, Honduras, El Salvador] (2001). Secretaría de Economía, <http://www.economia-snci.gob.mx/sphp,images/exporta/red_tratados.gif>, accessed 8 November 2003.
35 Quoted in 'US Relations Change Suddenly for Mexico,' *The Washington Post*, 21 September 2001, p. A32.
36 The 'Partnership for Prosperity' was launched by Presidents Fox and Bush during the latter's visit to Guanajuato, Mexico, in February 2001. Its purpose was to encourage the economic potential of every citizen 'so each may contribute fully to narrowing the

has found many obstacles on the way, the first being the terrorist attacks of September 11 that redefined the US foreign policy agenda. Mexico–US relations, however, had gone through significant changes before the 'new era'. Economic reform and the prospect of a trade agreement with the United States led Mexican governments to concentrate diplomatic efforts on the United States, leaving the usual – although ineffective – language of diversification in second place. Active bilateralism meant that a variety of actors and resources were involved in Mexico–US relations, and Mexican diplomacy, as mentioned above, adopted new methods, but with only one major purpose in mind.[37] Consequently, the Mexican government tried to isolate free trade negotiations from other issues such as drug trafficking, immigration and foreign policy. Mexican foreign policy became more cautious in multilateral fora, adopted a less anti-American stance, and preferred ad hoc initiatives such as the Rio Group, the Ibero-American Summits and the Group of Three.[38] Moreover, in the case of Central America, especially El Salvador and Guatemala, President Salinas, and later Zedillo, acted very much in consistency with US interests in the region: peaceful resolution and democratisation.[39]

---

    economic gaps between and within our societies'. The Partnership also aimed at moving beyond the bilateral trade relationship to 'create new and better opportunities for all of our citizens,' and to 'build on Mexico's strong regional development efforts, increased macroeconomic stability, and growing international trade and investment by developing new strategies to foster growth in less developed areas of Mexico'. It was a 'giant step' that reflected a new era of cooperation that would result in further economic and labour opportunities. <http://www.state.gov/p/wha/ci/mx/c7981.htm>, accessed 23 March 2004.

37 González, 'Foreign Policy Strategies,' p.154. By 1993, for example, the Mexican government had spent over 30 million USD in its pro-NAFTA campaign in the United States.

38 *Ibid.*, pp.153–54

39 Jorge I. Domínguez, *Widening Scholarly Horizons: Theoretical Approaches for the Study of US-Mexican Relations* (The David Rockefeller Center for Latin American Studies, Working Paper Series, no. 96-1). Cuba, however, was still an exception: despite Salinas's meetings with Cuban exiles, Mexico's official position regarding Castro's government continued to be that of non-intervention. See Ana Covarrubias, 'La política mexicana hacia Cuba durante el gobierno de Salinas de Gortari,' *Foro Internacional*, vol. 34, no. 4(138), October-December 1994, pp. 652–82.

NAFTA obviously modified the perception of what the United States represented to Mexico: the official discourse referred to it as a trade partner, with the emphasis put on partnership. In terms of the bilateral relationship, Domínguez and Fernández de Castro identify the following concrete consequences of NAFTA: a) it changed the governmental perception of bilateral affairs in Washington and Mexico City, and for the first time, both governments fostered integration instead of repressing it. Mexican and US leaders abandoned an ideological rhetoric and adopted a more pragmatic conflict-solving approach; b) the agreement institutionalised inter-governmental trade affairs and to a lesser extent, labour and environmental affairs.[40] The question, however, is: to what extent did the example of a formal dialogue and the establishment of trade dispute resolution mechanisms spill over to other issues in the bilateral relationship? Drug trafficking and immigration, for example, are two issues that have proved to be sources of conflict in the past, so a few words as to how they developed as the two countries became trade partners are not inappropriate.

As drug trafficking became a source of friction with the United States in the 1980s, it was clear that the Mexican State faced a double challenge to its authority and sovereignty: that of the drug dealers and that of foreign (US) police forces acting in Mexican territory. The Salinas government realised that any improvement in relations with the United States had to start by addressing the drug-trafficking problem, and this meant a new anti-drug policy that included extensive cooperation with that country.[41] Moreover, cooperation with the United States was a useful tool to solve problems that the Mexicans were incapable of solving, hence Mexico's new attitude regarding extradition and cooperation between the military

---

40 Domínguez and Fernández de Castro, *The United States and Mexico*.
41 For a detailed analysis of the changes in Mexican anti-drug policy, see María Celia Toro, 'Mexican policy against drugs: from deterring to embracing the United States,' 2003, unpublished manuscript. This section will rely mostly on this work, and on Jorge Chabat, 'Mexico's Foreign Policy in 1990: Electoral Sovereignty and Integration with the United States,' *Journal of Inter-American Studies and World Affairs*, vol. 33, no. 4, winter, 1991, pp. 1–25. I am grateful to Celia Toro for clarifying and expanding on some points in her article at my request.

of both countries.⁴² Mexico's disposition to collaborate with the United States preceded NAFTA, but once NAFTA became a reality, it provided a favourable framework for it to continue and it encouraged a process of institutionalisation. Some bilateral initiatives and efforts implemented since the late 1980s include: a special Anti-Money Laundering Unit (1988, UECLD, in Spanish), the Plenary Group on Law enforcement (1995), a High Level Contact Group for Drug Control (1996), a USA–Mexico Alliance against Drugs (1997) and Bilateral Border Task Forces. Mexico agreed, among other things, to coordinate maritime operations with the US Coast Guard, to allow surveillance operations by US ships and aircraft in Mexican seas and air space, to accept military support and training, and to admit 12 additional US law enforcement agents, 6 form the DEA and 6 from the FBI. Since 1996, applicants to Mexican organisations such as UECLD, or the Office of the Special Prosecutor for Crimes against Health and the Special Organised Crime Unit are scrutinised and tested with DEA and FBI support before they are admitted to join.

Despite all these efforts, President Salinas faced the kidnapping of Mexican doctor Humberto Álvarez Macháin in 1990 for his alleged participation in DEA's agent Enrique Camarena's assassination in 1985,⁴³ and President Zedillo had to deal with Operation Casablanca, an anti-money laundering investigation conducted by the US Custom Service partly in Mexican territory and without the Mexican government's knowledge, let alone authorisation. Álvarez Macháin was apparently kidnapped by Mexican police working for the DEA, and was taken to the United States to stand trial.⁴⁴ These cases, however, did not mean a return to the situation of the 1980s, and there have been other relative successes, such as the temporary suspension of the certification process in 2001, as a

---

42 Given Mexico's inefficient judicial system, for example, the extradition of drug dealers to the United States became a convenient arrangement for both countries. In January 2001, the Mexican Supreme Court ruled that the Mexican Executive had the legal right to extradite nationals. Toro, 'Mexican policy against drugs'.
43 Camarena was allegedly killed by drug-dealers but with the complicity (or impunity in any case) of the Mexican police.
44 Despite claims of extraterritoriality, the Álvarez Macháin case did not seem to disturb the cordiality that existed between Salinas and US President George Bush however. Chabat, 'Mexico's Foreign Policy in the 1990,' p. 9.

result of pressure from Latin American countries on the US government and the establishment of a Multilateral Evaluation Mechanism at the OAS. In the words of Celia Toro, the institutionalisation strategy lost momentum, however, and the US is less interested in maintaining it today. As to the role of NAFTA Toro argues that it certainly influenced the decisions taken by the Mexican government in the sense that it was necessary to avoid conflict with the United States and to establish a reputation as a reliable partner. NAFTA also provided a favourable context for the Mexican government to accommodate to US preferences, and made realignment more acceptable in Mexico. Mexico's drug policy reorientation was not, however, a result of NAFTA or a spill over effect: '[P]ut differently, Mexican policy against drugs would have changed in the same direction with or without NAFTA'.[45]

Immigration is a different story. Under strong pressure from Congress, President Clinton signed a series of Acts, and implemented a number of measures that reflected a tougher view towards illegal immigration (The Personal Responsibility and Work Opportunity Act, the Antiterrorism and Effective Death Penalty Act and the Illegal Immigration Reform and Immigrant Responsibility Act, 1996). In general terms, these Acts denied illegal immigrants certain social welfare benefits, increased surveillance at the border and watched more closely over US employers and forgers of documents for illegal immigrants.[46] Greater vigilance at the border forced Mexicans migrants to find other more dangerous crossing routes, resulting in a significant rise in the number of deaths.

In an attempt to find a way to manage the problem, Jorge Castañeda, Foreign Minister between 2000 and 2002, drafted a five point programme that placed illegal immigration on the agenda, presumably intending to get the US government actively involved and committed. The programme proposed: 1) to declare an amnesty for illegal immigrants already living in

---

45 Toro, 'Mexican policy against drugs'.
46 Manuel García y Griego and Mónica Verea Campos, 'Colaboración sin concordancia: La migración en la nueva agenda bilateral México-Estados Unidos,' in Mónica Verea Campos, Rafael Fernández de Castro and Sydney Weintraub (eds.), *Nueva agenda bilateral en la relación México-Estados Unidos* (Mexico: ITAM-UNAM/CISAN-FCE, 1998), pp. 107–34; Clint E. Smith, *Inevitable Partnership: Understanding Mexico-US Relations* (Boulder: Lynne Rienner, 2000).

the United States; 2) to increase the number of annual visas for Mexicans; 3) to establish a visiting workers' programme; 4) to improve border security; and 5) to promote economic development in the Mexican regions that provide the largest number of migrants.[47] It is not clear whether the US government was at any time willing to discuss such proposals, but it is true that the terrorist attacks of September 11 reduced the chances the programme might have had of being considered for debate (among other things, the INS became part of the newly created Department of Homeland Security, thus giving immigration a security dimension).[48] If we accept the view that the US government was not willing to press for the programme even before September 11, an improvement in Mexico–US relations resulting from NAFTA was irrelevant. Furthermore, why should have NAFTA been significant in any way since, after all, the US government refused to include immigration, or free movement of labour in the Treaty from the start? If, on the contrary, US authorities were willing to at least discuss Castañeda's proposal before the terrorist attacks, then one might perceive a change in US position. To what extent this change was a result of a gradual improvement in US–Mexico relations since the signature of NAFTA is a different question. President Bush's own recent proposal may be explained partly as a response to Mexico's insistence on the subject, or as a component of an electoral strategy.[49] In any case, any initiative, President Bush's or the Mexican government's, has a long way to go in US domestic politics before becoming a reality.

---

47 Jorge G. Castañeda, 'Los ejes de la política exterior de México,' *Nexos*, vol. 23, no. 288, December 2001, pp. 68–74.
48 The following quotation may be illustrative of the kind of debate, or perceptions, by a specific sector of public opinion in the United States about the nature of Mexico-US relations and the possibilities of reaching an immigration agreement: 'Mr. Bush was already going to have to overcome opposition within his own party for a migration pact. The Mexican stiff-arm on Iraq will only convince more Republicans that our neighbors to the south are more useful as political piñatas than as partners. And Mr. Bush will be even less inclined to risk his own prestige to help out Mr. Fox'. 'Our Friends at the U.N.,' *The Wall Street Journal*, 29 October 2002, p. A.22 (editorial).
49 At the beginning of January 2004, President Bush announced an immigration proposal that recognised the benefits provided by immigrants to the US economy, and suggested the convenience of encouraging a programme for foreign temporary workers, among other things.

US–Mexican relations have been, and will always be, complex and difficult to manage, and they can be best understood in terms of cycles or moments, rather than grand strategies leading to 'new eras'. Relations under Salinas, Zedillo and Fox were not close to what they were under López Portillo or de la Madrid, and although it is difficult to determine events as signs of deterioration in relations, it might be worth noting that neither Salinas nor Zedillo had to deal with issues such as Operation Intercept, the Helms Congressional hearings or rows over foreign policy issues, such as Contadora.[50] There are various explanations for this: domestic transformations in Mexico and the fact that there have not been major issues at the international level likely to promote serious disagreements between the two governments. At the same time, however, Fox and Castañeda's hope for a 'strategic relationship' with the United States has not materialised. The war in Iraq was Fox's first test and the result seems to have been distance rather than conflict. As González argues, 'despite the fact that NAFTA opened a new era of bilateral co-operation and institutional dialogue, collaboration between the two countries remains segmented and the extent of mutual confidence limited'.[51]

Domestic issues

One might look at the consequences of political divergence between the United States and Mexico during de la Madrid's *sexenio* as incipient 'internationalisation' of the discussion of Mexico's political and social problems, let alone economics. This process of internationalisation was both forced and voluntary. The first case is illustrated by a sudden interest in Mexico's politics within the United States, to a large extent as a consequence of the assassination of Enrique Camarena. This event triggered a series of debates about corruption and the lack of an efficient judicial system in Mexico, and even electoral fraud and the absence of democracy. TV programmes and the Helms Congressional hearings portrayed a country

---

50 Zedillo's major disagreement with the United States was the Helms-Burton Law, but it did not have a serious negative impact on relations as a whole.
51 González, 'Foreign Policy Strategies,' p. 175

on the verge of chaos.⁵² Equally important was the fact that Americas Watch and Amnesty International (AI) for the first time issued reports on the situation of human rights in Mexico in 1984 and 1986, respectively. Americas Watch informed on the government's treatment of Guatemalan refugees, and AI on rural violence.⁵³

With regard to the 'voluntary process of internationalisation', Mexican actors turned to foreign actors to denounce electoral fraud; a good example is the PAN's complaints at the inter-American Commission on Human Rights (IACHR) regarding electoral irregularities (including the legislative elections in Chihuahua in 1985, municipal elections in the capital of the state of Durango in 1986, elections for the governorship of Chihuahua in 1986, and legislative and municipal elections in the state of Mexico in 1990).⁵⁴ According to Jorge Chabat, Washington's unusual

52 Jorge Chabat, 'La política exterior de Miguel de la Madrid: las paradojas de la modernización en un mundo interdependiente,' in Carlos Bazdresch, Nisso Bucay, Soledad Loaeza and Nora Lustig (eds.), *México: ajuste y crisis* (Mexico: Fondo de Cultura Económica, 1992); Francisco Gil Villegas, 'La nueva relación especial de México y Estados Unidos durante 1990: cordialidad en medio de situaciones conflictivas,' in Gustavo Vega (ed.), *México-Estados Unidos 1990* (Mexico: El Colegio de México, 1992); Sergio Aguayo, '1986: el creciente interés por México en Estados Unidos,' in Gerardo Bueno (ed.), *México-Estados Unidos, 1986* (Mexico: El Colegio de México, 1987), pp. 99–123; Blanca Torres, 'La visión estadounidense de las elecciones de 1985: ¿presión de coyuntura o preocupación de largo plazo?,' in Székely (ed.), *México-Estados Unidos*, pp. 45–62.
53 Kathryn Sikkink, 'Human rights, principled issued-networks, and sovereignty in Latin America,' *International Organization*, vol. 47, no. 3, summer 1993, p. 431.
54 The IACHR report was favourable to the PAN by expressing concerns over violations of human rights in those elections. The Mexican government reacted strongly to this, arguing that the Commission lacked the 'competence to pass judgement on electoral processes of a given country or to deal with actions that fall within the domain reserved to each State, and that it was violating the principle of non-intervention'. If a 'State agreed to submit itself to international jurisdiction with respect to the election of its political bodies, a State would cease to be sovereign'. The IACHR responded in turn affirming that the government's position was unfounded, and that to make effective the political rights contained in the American Convention of Human Rights, Mexico's internal electoral law needed to be reformed. See Chabat, 'Mexico's Foreign Policy in 1990,' p. 11; Sikkink, 'Human rights,' p. 432; Ana Covarrubias, 'El ámbito internacional y el proceso de cambio político en México,' in Reynaldo Yunuen Ortega Ortiz (ed.), *Caminos a la democracia* (Mexico: El Colegio de México, 2001), pp. 356–38.

attention to Mexico in the 1980s was partly a result of what was happening in Central America, – the idea that the 'communist virus' might contaminate Mexico, and the difficulty to exempt Mexico from a policy of promoting democracy in the isthmus – but, more importantly, through an increasing instability in Mexico reflected in a legitimacy crisis in its political system.[55]

Years later Salinas deliberately placed Mexico on the world stage in his attempt to portray a country on its way to 'modernity' worth being a NAFTA and an OECD member.[56] Once this outward-looking process started, however, it could not be stopped, went beyond the economic sphere, and in time had unintended and unexpected consequences for Mexican governments, as the Zapatista uprising illustrates. In general, however, President Salinas tried to avoid external interference in the domestic political sphere, and Mexico's foreign policy remained a useful tool with which to do so. His government refused to support the 'new' OAS that intended to actively advance democracy and the protection of human rights in member states,[57] and despite the dominant place of democracy in the international agenda, NAFTA did not include a democratic clause.[58] At the UN World Conference on Human Rights in Vienna in June 1993, for example, Mexico was among those countries that rejected the idea of the universality of human rights,[59] and opposed the creation of the post of High Commissioner for Human Rights on the basis of national

---

55 Chabat, 'Mexico's Foreign Policy in 1990,' p. 10.
56 According to President Salinas, the modernisation process implied a re-organisation of the country to increase its strength, 'through unity, democracy, and social justice, as the only way to affirm Mexico's sovereignty and have a greater presence in the modern world'. Carlos Salinas de Gortari, 'Primer informe de gobierno,' *Comercio Exterior*, vol. 39, no. 11, November 1989, p. 932.
57 Some of the documents rejected by the Mexican government for violating non-intervention were the Santiago Commitment (1991), Resolution 1080 (1991), the Washington (1992) and Managua (1993) Protocols. These documents established the need and the procedures for an active promotion of democracy and protection of human rights in the OAS members.
58 Surely not because Salinas did not want to; after all, NAFTA was a trade agreement and the leaders of both countries must have recognised that such a clause was not desirable by any party. The agreement concluded with the EU in 2000 did include a democratic clause.
59 'Threats and jeers bode ill for conference harmony,' *The Times*, 14 June 1993.

sovereignty. Mexico's position on that occasion was 'to combine national sovereignty with global consensus and protect the very same bases upon which the community of nations is built'.[60] That is, Mexico supported international cooperation to protect human rights but always taking into account the national perspective; the protection of human rights should be impartial, objective and not selective, and it should not become the means to export certain models of political or economic organisation.[61]

The Salinas government, nevertheless, clearly perceived that the issue of human rights had to be addressed, and acted accordingly on a few occasions. The National Human Rights Commission was created in 1990, according to Sikkink, as a pre-emptive move by the Salinas government to control the human rights problem in the context of increasing criticism. In 1990, for example, Americas Watch had issued a report on human rights conditions in Mexico, and the US Congress also held hearings on the subject for the first time. Sikkink argues that the creation of the Commission reflected the government's concern that Mexico might be subject to heightened scrutiny from the US administration and Congress in the context of future free trade negotiations.[62] By the end of his term, and in a more complicated context after the Zapatista uprising and the assassination of PRI presidential candidate Luis Donaldo Colosio, Salinas accepted what his government had tried to avoid so far: foreign electoral monitoring.[63] The government's decision to allow the presence of *visitantes internacionales* in the 1994 elections was the response to a critical domestic situation, but

---

60 'Derechos humanos: incorporan a México al club de los "renegados",' *Proceso*, no. 869, June 28, 1993, pp. 40–41.
61 *Ibid*. By the end of the year, however, Mexico enthusiastically endorsed the creation of the High Commissioner Office.
62 Sikkink, 'Human rights,', pp. 432–3. Sikkink's argues that Salinas's strategy was to take pre-emptive measures to project the image of his administration's concern over human rights. Before meeting with President-elect Bill Clinton, Salinas appointed Jorge Carpizo, a former Supreme Court Justice and president of the NCHR as Attorney General.
63 In 1990, for example, Fernando Solana, Minister of Foreign Affairs, had declared that the problems of democracy would be resolved by the Mexicans 'and not by importing specialised observers from Atlanta or Milwaukee to tell us how to do things,' *La Jornada*, 5 December 1990, p. 1, quoted by Chabat, 'Mexico's Foreign Policy in 1990,' p. 14.

also to constant requests from US NGOs, such as the Carter Centre and the National Democratic Institute. Moreover, as electoral tendencies seemed to favour the PRI, the government thought foreign observers might legitimate the election results.[64]

In effect, democracy and human rights in Mexico rapidly became the subject of international scrutiny, and Mexican authorities gradually accepted, welcomed and encouraged it. Zedillo's *sexenio* illustrates well the tension between continuity and change: as it progressed, the government took a series of concrete steps that suggested a more deliberate move towards accepting a foreign presence and opinions about what was previously thought of as 'strictly domestic issues'. The Human Rights Inter-American Commission, visited Mexico in 1996 at the government's invitation; the government recognised the jurisdiction of the Inter-American Human Rights Court in 1998, signed the International Penal Court Statute and concluded an Economic Partnership, Political Co-ordination and Cooperation Agreement with the EU that included a democratic clause. UN representatives such as Kofi Annan, Mary Robinson, Nigel Rodley and Asma Jahangir also visited the country at the Mexican authorities' invitation. José Ángel Gurría, Foreign Minister at the time, openly expressed that these invitations were part of the government's new attitude towards human rights and democracy, acknowledging that in the past, Mexican authorities had maintained that the purpose of international organisations was to *question the country* [sic].[65] Furthermore, an inter-Ministerial Commission was created at the end of 1997 to attend to Mexico's international commitments in the field of human rights. The creation of the Commission was justified through the existence of an international community that had strengthened the universal respect of human rights through a series of international instruments, and because Mexico's adherence to many international treaties on the subject demonstrated its support to the struggle in favour of human rights ('by conviction of its own people'). Moreover, one of the aims of the Plan Nacional de Desarrollo 1995–2000 was the implementation of the rule of law,

---

64 Raúl Benítez Manaut, 'La ONU en México: elecciones presidenciales de 1994,' *Foro Internacional*, vol. 36, no. 3(145), July-September, 1996, pp.
65 *La Jornada*, 19 August 1997, pp.1, 6. Emphasis added.

something that would only be possible by fully respecting human rights. Two of the Commission's purposes were to make sure Mexico complied with its international commitments, and to recommend policies to make international treaties effective within the country.[66]

The evidence, therefore, suggests that Zedillo's policy in the field of human rights was shaped by taking the international agenda and its consequences on Mexico as major points of reference.[67] This did not mean, however, that the government welcomed action or involvement from any external actor: Mexican authorities contested international NGOs' criticism and resisted their activities in the country. President Zedillo refused to meet AI Secretary General, Pierre Sané (1997), and immigration authorities enforced strict new rules for issuing visas to foreign human rights observers (1998).[68] In this way, Zedillo's policy may be understood as a 'protected opening' by which the government reinforced its authority and recognised states (even if acting through international organisations) as the only legitimate actors in the international system. Such an opening did, however, result in visible and concrete changes in foreign policy.

Change had to be at the top of the agenda of Vicente Fox's government. In his first annual report, President Fox enumerated five major 'axes' that would guide his government's foreign policy: 1) to show to the

---

66 Interestingly, a representative of SRE would preside over the Commission, and the other permanent members would be representatives from the Ministry of Interior, National Defence and the Navy. Representatives from the General Attorney's Office, *Procuraduría General de la República*, and the Human Rights National Commission would be permanent guests, and the Commission's president was free to invite any other guests if convenient. 'Acuerdo por el que se constituye la Comisión Intersecretarial para la atención de los compromisos internacionales de México en materia de derechos humanos'< http://info4.juridicas.unam.mx/ijure/nrm/1/71/1.htm?s=iste>, accessed 28 January 2004.

67 Admittedly, more research needs to be done to establish if, and how, such an external influence acted through national organisations. That is, whether this would be a case of what Kathryn Sikkink and Margaret Keck call the 'boomerang pattern'. *Activists beyond Borders. Advocacy Networks in International Politics* (Ithaca: Cornell University Press, 1998), pp. 12–13.

68 Among other things, the law required the applicants to demonstrate the seriousness of the organisations they represented, and visits could last no more than ten days. NGOs such as AI and Human Rights Watch Americas reacted very strongly. See Covarrubias, 'El ámbito internacional y el proceso de cambio político en México,' pp. 366–8.

world the consolidation of Mexico's democratic institutions, and to project the image of a plural, transparent, safe and culturally dynamic country; 2) to support and promote in an active and committed way the respect and defence of human rights in the world; 3) to defend democracy as the only kind of government that can guarantee the peoples' welfare; 4) to have a more active role in the construction of the international system of the new millennium; 5) to promote sustainable economic development.[69] Fox's government initially designed and implemented an *active* foreign policy. With regard to human rights, it is worth noting that the first agreement signed by the new government on 2 December 2000 was the Agreement on Technical Assistance in Human Rights Matters with the UN High Commissioner for Human Rights (UNHCHR); a liaison office to implement the agreement was opened in Mexico City in July 2002. The Ministry of Foreign Affairs even created a high level office (*subsecretaría*) for human rights, thereby illustrating that human rights were recognised as 'intermestic' issues and had a legitimate place in foreign policy[70] and, more importantly, human rights were recognised as universal and indivisible. The Mexican government has continued to welcome representatives from international organisations to assess the state of human rights in the country and has also opened the door to NGOs (the visa legislation for foreign observers has been repealed). Moreover, the Mexican government even damaged its relations with Cuba by taking the democratic and human rights banner at the UN Human Rights Commission in Geneva, where it voted in favour of resolutions calling for an improvement in, or at least an assessment of, the situation in Cuba.[71]

In brief, the government of Vicente Fox has enthusiastically endorsed international political tendencies: the link between free trade and democracy was reaffirmed in the Quebec Declaration (2001) and the

---

69 Mexico, Presidente, Vicente Fox, *Primer Informe de Gobierno*, 2001; Castañeda, 'Los ejes de la política exterior de México,' and an interview in *Arcana*, no. 8, December 2001, pp. 20–5.
70 The Subsecretaría, however, was eliminated in 2003 and the Subsecretaría de Asuntos Globales is now in charge of human rights issues.
71 The Mexican government – rather cautiously – expressed its concern over Cuba's lack of political opening and the situation of human rights oin the island from the beginning of the 1990s, and Fox's government continued such policy more assertively.

Inter-American Democratic Charter (2001). The international terms of reference, however, changed as terrorism and security rose to the top of the US – and international – agenda, and it is not clear whether or how the Mexican government might reorient its foreign policy accordingly.

IV New and active foreign policies: ruptures and *alternancias*

Mexico's *new* foreign policy, however distinctive, is not entirely new, nor is it Mexico's *active* foreign policy. Luis Echeverría pursued a *new and active* foreign policy, and López Portillo and Salinas's foreign policies were not exactly 'inactive'. A detailed comparison between these periods would certainly be a very productive exercise but, given space restrictions, the analysis will be limited to only two presidents: Luis Echeverría and Vicente Fox. In both cases, and despite clear differences in domestic and international contexts, rhetoric, strategies and even objectives are similar, and both leaders wanted openly to signal a rupture with the previous government – or regime – in Fox's case. Internationally, Echeverría acted within détente whereas Fox's government has had to manage different expressions of unipolarity.

Interestingly, Echeverría's foreign policy resorted to the language of activity, democracy and human rights, and intended to have an influence on the international system. 'Mexico – according to Echeverría – cannot grow in isolation. Nothing that happens beyond our borders can be alien to us and isolation is impossible in an era of increasing interdependence ... We need to multiply and intensify our relations with all countries...'[72] In six years, Echeverría made twelve international trips, visiting 36 countries,[73] he was also the first Mexican president to visit socialist Cuba and the USSR, attended the OAS on one occasion and the UN twice, and welcomed more than 30 heads of state or other high-level foreign officials. Mexico increased the number of countries with which it had diplomatic relations from 67 to 129, and signed 160 international agreements or treaties.[74]

72 Mexico, Presidente, Luis Echeverría Álvarez, *Segundo Informe de Gobierno*, 1972.
73 *Ibid*. Europe (9), Asia (4), Africa and the Middle East (9), and Latin America (14).
74 Ojeda, *México*, p. 64; Mexico, Presidente, Luis Echeverría Álvarez, *Sexto Informe de Gobierno*, 1976, p. 125.

Echeverría's active foreign policy took shape in a context of economic and political difficulties: on the one hand, the government had to reactivate the economy as the economic model based on ISI had reached a stalemate;[75] on the other, it had to deal with internal divisions in the PRI and with social discontent. Therefore, one of Echeverría's initial objectives was to strengthen economic growth by diversifying Mexico's economic external relations. To do this, the government concentrated its efforts on promoting exports and looking for new international markets. Echeverría's commercial diplomacy, however, faced a major obstacle in August 1971 when the US government imposed a 10 per cent surcharge on all its imports and refused to exempt Mexican products on the basis of an alleged 'special relationship' between the two countries. Echeverría's response was the design of a New International Economic Order, NIEO, to 'correct inequalities and redress existing injustices, [and to] eliminate the widening gap between the developed and the developing countries and ensure steadily accelerating economic and social development and peace and justice ...'[76]

The Charter of Economic Rights and Duties of States was the instrument to promote the NIEO and became an end in itself for Mexican foreign policy. In order to obtain support for the Charter, Echeverría adopted a Third World orientation which implied, for example, rapprochement with Asian and African countries and, in Latin America, with Cuba, given Castro's leading position in the Third World movement. Echeverría's *tercermundismo* was intended to expand Mexico's relations with a great number of countries, to diversify markets and economic and political

---

75 The first phase of import substitution of consumer goods had been completed and a second stage of intermediate and capital goods had to begin. To do so, the Mexican economy required great sums of investment and new technology, which it did not have. Moreover, low quality and high prices had made it difficult for Mexican goods to compete in the international market. Additionally, external debt became a heavier burden and sources of income, such as tourism and border transactions, were no longer providing sufficient resources to balance the foreign trade deficit. Ojeda, *México,* pp. 48–49. See also Carlos Rico, *Hacia la globalización. México y el mundo: historia de sus relaciones exteriores,* vol. IX (Mexico: Senado de la República, 2000. Series ed. by Blanca Torres and Roberta Lajous), pp. 22–4.
76 'Declaration on the Establishment of a New International Economic Order,' *Yearbook of the United Nations,* 1974, vol. 28, p. 324.

interests, and to increase the negotiating power of less developed areas before the world powers.[77] The government of Mexico endorsed different initiatives in the region, such as the Latin American Economic System, SELA, as a further means of strengthening the presence of Latin American countries in the world economy.

Foreign policy, however, also had a very strong political content. Echeverría had to deal with the legacy of repression and political divisions of the Gustavo Díaz Ordaz's *sexenio*, namely the October 1968 violent clash between government forces and students at the Tlatelolco square (when Echeverría himself was minister of interior). One of the major consequences of October 1968 was that the left and the leftist sector of the governing party were alienated, and some of them turned to guerrilla activities. In addition, the PRI had been further weakened by internal divisions between those who wanted a more democratic party and those who resisted change.[78] In brief, Mexico's traditional political stability was at risk; according to Barry Carr, the hegemonic scope of the Revolution's ideology appeared to crumble.[79] In this troubled political scenario, Echeverría decided to reintegrate leftist forces to political life[80] and revitalise the regime by underlining its nationalist and progressive stands. Foreign policy could be a very useful instrument to underline the regime's progressive and tolerant features, and it was not costly. Ideological pluralism in international politics became the counterpart of a 'democratic opening' by which Mexican authorities sought to promote criticism and self-criticism of the government, tolerance, and dialogue with dissident sectors.[81] The Echeverría government established diplomatic relations with countries of various ideological orientations and actively promoted the adoption of

---

77 Eugenio Anguiano, 'México y el Tercer Mundo: racionalización de una posición,' *Foro Internacional*, vol. 18, no. 1(69), July-September 1977, p. 180.
78 The PRI's General Secretary Carlos Madrazo had proposed the democratisation of the PRI through a primary election. Madrazo was killed in an air crash which allegedly was not an accident. Abstention increased in the 1970 and 1973 elections, and the main opposition party, PAN, had already gained more votes in the 1970 Presidential election. See Ojeda, *México*, pp. 51–2; Barry Carr, *La izquierda mexicana a través del siglo XX* (Mexico: ERA, 1996), p. 276.
79 Carr, *La izquierda mexicana*, p. 276.
80 Except for the guerrilla, which was mostly repressed.
81 Ojeda, *México*, p. 53.

political pluralism at the OAS. Its Third World orientation was consistent and helpful in this task.

As part of the strategy, the Mexican government approached Cuba and Allende's Chile. A marked improvement in relations with Cuba was a convenient instrument to underline the nationalistic and progressive nature of the Mexican regime. Allende's Chile, on the other hand, was perhaps more valuable in terms of Echeverría's domestic purposes as it represented democracy and self-determination. At a time when the actions of guerrillas were becoming increasingly visible in Mexico, the idea of change through democratic means was very useful.[82] Interestingly, the Chilean coup d'état was an opportunity to stress the importance of human rights for the Mexican government: it condemned human rights violations in Chile, as well as any dictatorial persecution for political reasons. In an unusual move for Mexican diplomacy, relations with Chile were severed in 1974. On the same basis, of the inadmissibility of human rights violations, the Mexican government refused to establish diplomatic relations with South Africa and Rhodesia, and ultimately also broke relations with Spain. With regard to the Spanish case, Echeverría's declarations are illustrative: '[I]n defence of human rights and worried about the threat to peace, we denounced at the United Nations the serious events that took place in Spain last year (the assassination of Basque dissidents). We are carefully watching the democratisation process in Spain and we hope, together with the progressive sectors of this nation, that its march is accelerated'.[83] The Mexican government went as far as to request a UN Security Council meeting that would in turn ask the General Assembly to expel Spain from the organisation for the violation of human rights. The UN Security Council did not consider Mexico's request, and Echeverría later decided to stop all communications with Spain. To re-establish relations with Spain – Echeverría said – Mexico needed to see certain conditions including a parliament with representation of all political parties, freedom of the press, freedom of prisoners, and the return of émigrés to Spain.[84] As in the case of Chile, Echeverría praised Mexico's

82 Carlos Arriola, 'El acercamiento mexicano-chileno,' *Foro Internacional*, vol. 14, no. 4, April-June, 1974, pp. 507–47.
83 Quoted by Shapira, 'La política exterior de México,' p. 76.
84 Mexico, Presidente, Luis Echeverría Álvarez, *Sexto Informe de Gobierno*, 1976, p. 130.

asylum policy as a defence of human rights.[85]

Vicente Fox, in turn, proposed an active foreign policy, including an economic diplomacy, before he took power.[86] In an article in a special issue of *Foreign Affairs en Español,* Fox stated that democracy and integral development were linked, but more interestingly he identified Mexico's emerging democracy as the condition that allowed the country to participate more actively in the international arena.[87] Contrary to the case of Echeverría, Fox did not face any major crisis as he came to power, but being the government of *la alternancia,* democracy and human rights found a central place in domestic and foreign policy. Like the case of Echeverría, Fox's government stated that Mexico had the responsibility of actively participating in the making of a new international system, although the emphasis this time was on emerging universal rules such as the protection of human rights. Mexico should influence or profit from the inevitable transformations in the international environment.

By November 2003 President Fox had made at least 29 international trips visiting around 45 different countries, and had welcomed more than 9 high level foreign officials. Mexico occupied a non-permanent seat at the United Nations Security Council and hosted the UN Conference on Financing for Development and the APEC summit in 2002, the WTO summit in 2003, and the Special Summit of the Americas in January 2004 (and the EU–LA summit in May of 2004). The Office for the Free Trade of the Americas is located in Mexico, and the signature of the UN Convention against Corruption took place in Mérida, Yucatán, in December 2003.[88]

The domestic and international contexts in which President Fox is acting are obviously different from those that Echeverría had to face: among other things, Mexico is a formal trade partner of the United States and Canada, and the PRI is no longer the party in power. Fox, as already

---

85 *Ibid.*
86 See <www.fox2000.org.mx>, accessed February 2002.
87 Vicente Fox, 'La diplomacia económica de México,' *Foreign Affairs en Español*, special edition, December 2000, pp. 8–9, 16.
88 <http://www.sre.gob.mx/acerca/giras/>, accessed 8 November 2003. For all the activities of the Mexican government in the field of foreign policy see <http://comovamos.presidencia.gob.mx>, accessed 28 January 2004.

mentioned, highlighted an economic diplomacy before he took office but, contrary to Echeverría, not to promote major transformations in Mexico's domestic economy, or as a reaction to an adverse international system. It is more perhaps a means to confirm that Mexico's economic orientation is consistent with tendencies prevailing at the international level, and of course an instrument to encourage growth. The idea, according to Fox, is to benefit from globalisation, not to fight against it.[89] Finally, despite NAFTA and its belonging to the OECD, the Mexican government recognises the position of the country as less developed and, once again, intends to have a leading role, by presenting itself as a bridge between industrialised and less developed countries. In this spirit, Mexico hosted the UN Conference on Financing for Development and the WTO summit.

Another economic project proposed at the beginning of Fox's *sexenio* was the '*Plan Puebla-Panamá*', PPP, which was intended to promote development in the south and south-east regions of Mexico and the Central American countries. Funded by public and private, national and international sources, the Plan proposed to turn the region into a 'development pole' profiting by the availability of labour and natural resources.[90] This was a major foreign policy initiative towards the Central American countries that has not progressed much.[91]

As important as economic foreign policy, or perhaps more so, is Fox's 'political' policy. Foreign policy initiatives in the field of human rights have already been mentioned but it is worth emphasising that the promotion and defence of human rights is a declared 'fundamental principle' guiding Mexico's foreign policy. In addition to the UNHCHR office in Mexico, the government reports the visit of 15 representatives of human rights organisations to the country.[92]

The comparison of Echeverría and Fox's foreign policy is interesting in terms of identifying the sources of foreign policy in various ways. Echeverría's foreign policy was perceived in the framework of general reforms and was designed to revitalise the political system by giving it back

---

89 Fox, 'La diplomacia económica de México,' pp. 10–15.
90 See <http://www.presidencia.gob.mx>, accessed 8 November 2003.
91 <http://comovamos.presidencia.gob.mx>, accessed 28 January 2004.
92 10 from the United Nations, 4 from the IACHR and 1 from AI. <http://comovamos.presidencia.gob.mx>, accessed 28 January 2004.

part of its old progressive and nationalist character. In addition to economic objectives, it pursued national unity through reconciliation with dissident groups to return to stability and public peace.[93] Fox places the emphasis on projecting new values but such projection is, at the same time, an instrument to consolidate those values within the country. The domestic dimension of foreign policy is, in both cases, undeniable. On the other hand, the international system did not seem to have 'forced' either of them to shape their foreign policies in the way they did, but it provided a strong incentive.

---

93 Ojeda, *Alcances y límites*, p. 168.

V Reflections on change: how new is new, how active is active, and how different can it get?

Strictly speaking, all foreign policies originate domestically. What the Mexican case may offer, however, is a more detailed view of what the domestic variable may mean, precisely because of Mexico's position in the world as a country that is relatively vulnerable to outside events and pressures, but that at the same time can choose not to be deeply involved in international politics. In other words, Mexico does not have global interests to defend in Vietnam, Kosovo or Iraq, for example, but the power of its northern neighbour, the clash of ideologies or trends in the international economy do have an impact on the country that may, in turn, translate into foreign policy. In this sense, a view of what happens inside the country contributes to explaining why Mexican governments choose to act internationally when they do and in the ways they do, and whether they pursue domestic or international goals. This does not mean that Mexico's is, or has been, a rational and well-designed policy all the time, but it does remind us of the crucial issue of choice.

There is no doubt that the economic and financial crisis of the 1980s was primarily domestic (if with unquestionable foreign links) but the 'solution' that brought about change came mostly from abroad; imposition may be a strong word but the lack of alternatives and the seriousness of the situation left little option but to follow what external actors requested. President Salinas, however, also constrained by the international resources available, or not, thought of change as a more deliberate strategy with a single purpose, the conclusion of NAFTA, and it was not a sudden reaction to a domestic or external crisis. The role of the international system is a bit tricky: did it induce this strategy or did it only help to make it successful? The answer should be both: the ideas of free trade and open economies had been on the international agenda for some years (Canada and the United States had already signed a free trade agreement), as well as the expectation that international institutions would foster cooperation among countries. By joining international trends, Mexico's strategy increased its chances of being successful, and a domestic political system that gave the President and his cabinet a great capacity to act and minimise opposition, and a majority in Congress, assured such success. However, an interesting aspect of Salinas's NAFTA strategy was that it intended to lock-in domestic reforms thus making a foreign policy initiative more directly a domestic policy. This is nothing new in Mexican – or other countries'– foreign policy, but it certainly enriches foreign policy analysis: is it the source or the purpose (intended audience) which is domestic or international? Further, how do they relate to each other: foreign policy originates domestically for domestic or for external purposes? These questions will be further explored below; suffice it to underline now the role of foreign policy as an instrument of domestic politics.

The governments of Ernesto Zedillo and Vicente Fox consolidated and expanded Mexico's new economic foreign policy if for no other reason than because NAFTA already existed, and despite its shortcomings no alternative has been found. Commercial diplomacy always responds to any country's needs and interests, but after the 1980s, it took a larger space in Mexican foreign policy and acquired predominance and visibility. Trade initiatives, in turn, required a more active foreign policy and a greater involvement of the country in the world, and an increase in the number of actors, national and international, taking part in Mexico's external relations.

Politically speaking, however, the 1980s and early 1990s did not witness major changes in Mexican foreign policy. Ideas such as the promotion of democracy and the protection of human rights also had an increasingly prominent place in the international agenda,[94] but Mexican governments refused to embrace them: there were strong accusations of US interference in domestic affairs during de la Madrid's term, as there was no democratic clause in NAFTA and no support for the idea of the OAS actively promoting democracy and human rights. It was only after the 1994 election, and in a post-*Zapatismo*, post-Colosio and post-Ruiz Massieu[95] context

---

94 The process of democratisation in some Latin American countries had already started.
95 José Francisco Ruiz Massieu was the Secretary General of the PRI when he was assassinated in September 1994 in Mexico City.

that Zedillo's government started to act more forcefully according to international trends on those subjects, surely as a response to an increasing and strong international criticism generated by these events – a response that contrasts to that of de la Madrid. Foreign policy, once more, seemed to be a useful tool to point in the direction of change: Zedillo's government turned to the inter-American system and the UN; his government endorsed the creation of the IPC and consented to the inclusion of a democratic clause in the treaty signed with the EU, but was cautious not to allow a complete 'internationalisation' of internal problems and tried to retain as much control over domestic issues as possible. International organisations were legitimate interlocutors, but not NGOs.

The ultimate cause that prompted President Zedillo to implement changes in foreign policy in the field of human rights was obviously domestic, and although it was not new (the poor state of human rights in Mexico was known long before), there was a greater sense of urgency than, for example, during Salinas's term before the Zapatista uprising. In other words, domestic circumstances from January 1994 onwards made the country more vulnerable to a more resolute incursion from *the outside*. Kathryn Sikkink would identify the attention that the human rights international network paid to Mexico as the main explanatory variable, an argument that can be supported by the fact that there was a quick response, most visible in foreign policy, by the Mexican government. Zedillo's *sexenio* would be a clear case of what Sikkink refers to as the transition from denial to lip service: 'denial of the legitimacy and refusal to cooperate with any international human rights pressures or interventions' to the acceptance of 'the legitimacy of international human rights practices, as evidenced by its statements in international forums, ratification of the relevant human rights treaties, and cooperation with international human rights organizations', but without taking the following step of modifying domestic practices.[96] Was change an imposition from *the outside*? Not necessarily, if one considers social and political processes within the country: the mid-term elections of 1997 signalled the extent of domestic transformations, at least at the electoral level, and Mexican authorities might have calculated that the PRI-government could not resist change

---

96 Sikkink, 'Human Rights,' p. 435 (n. 76).

for much longer.⁹⁷ Was *the outside* an incentive? Yes, a very potent one. On the other hand, if leadership is also a valid explanatory variable, did Zedillo act expecting to be internationally recognised as the historical figure who led Mexico to democracy? ⁹⁸ In brief, Zedillo's foreign policy regarding human rights –and to a lesser extent democracy – originated from a domestic problem and had external purposes (in the sense of an improved external image), but not exclusively.

President Fox's is more clearly a case of foreign policy designed to be an instrument of domestic politics, at least at the beginning of his *sexenio*. According to former Minister Castañeda, foreign policy would promote and consolidate domestic reforms: '[T]he priorities of our international policy are not only the consequence, but also the cause of this process of renovation [democratic transition], and may contribute in a decisive way to supporting internal change'.⁹⁹ Moreover, Castañeda underlined that the universal principles and the values that Fox's government professed in international fora 'impose on us the obligation of acting congruently in our domestic regime'. The cause for human rights was certainly the best illustration of '[T]his complex game between foreign policy and domestic change'.¹⁰⁰

---

97 The PRI lost 5.5 million votes with respect to 1994, a greater fall than expected, and it lost the majority in Congress. More importantly, the PRD won Mexico City's government. See Rafael Segovia, 'La resistencia al cambio,' in Ortega, *Caminos a la democracia*, pp. 133–5. Once again, only a closer look at the interaction between specific domestic and foreign actors at different times will clarify this suggestion. Such an exercise and the question of whether the kind of sources explains the nature of foreign policy (is it active because it has domestic/external origin or purpose?) may constitute an interesting research agenda for the future.

98 Just as Echeverría is said to have used his Third World policy as a means to become the UN Secretary General.

99 Jorge G. Castañeda, 'Política exterior y cambio democrático,' *Reforma*, 12 July 2002, <http://busquedas.gruporeforma.com/utilerias/imdservicios3W.DLL?JSearchformat SP...>, accessed 22 March 2004. This would represent the last stage of the continuum proposed by Sikkink; that is, reconstituted sovereignty of the state, or the recognition of the legitimacy of human rights concerns and willingness to cooperate. In this case, states respond concretely to international pressures and, more importantly, actually modify domestic human rights practices. 'Human Rights,' p. 415.

100 Castañeda, 'Política exterior'. Castañeda was firm that one of the main objectives of foreign policy was to consolidate democratic change and political *alternancia* in Mexico. In his words: '*De ahí la importancia que hoy tiene para México [...] el anclaje que la política exterior provee al cambio interno...*'

This view of foreign policy takes the argument closer to the 'regime type' or 'regime change' explanations which incorporate the idea of projecting values. Explicitly, Fox's foreign policy has intended to demonstrate the degree of change in the country: a *new* foreign policy for a *new* Mexico. In this case, foreign policy would theoretically be the continuation of domestic politics. Whether this is really the case with regards to Mexico's current foreign policy is difficult to say; any argument in that direction would need to first establish if Mexico is indeed a consolidated democracy, and this, we know, is no easy task. On the other hand, it is worth looking inside Mexico for there is no doubt that what happens there is increasingly more relevant to foreign policy: the links between internal and international organisations, governmental or not, are stronger; Congress and public opinion now more frequently discuss international matters and foreign policy; and, in effect, a visible, *active* foreign policy has had an impact in terms of underlining discrepancies between domestic and international policy if only because it attracts public attention.[101] Are we therefore witnessing a *new* foreign policy after all? Is this the continuation or the culmination of a process? Is this process considered progress? Or is Mexican foreign policy today just a different expression of old concerns, interests and limitations? The questions in the subtitle of this section of this paper may help address these issues.

How *new* is *new*? The idea of 'new' is of course not new but it is interesting to see why Mexican governments have resorted to it. It obviously suggests breaking with the past but certain ruptures have been more definite and have had more long term consequences than others. If we agree that the most significant and permanent change in foreign policy first took place in the economic sphere in the 1980s and 1990s, then de la Madrid and Salinas should hold the title of innovators (even when de la Madrid's policy was perhaps more a series of reactions than a well designed strategy). Since foreign policy may also be seen as a process, it would, however, be safer to argue that Mexican foreign policy has gradually incorporated new topics, or has redefined and changed the hierarchy of

---

101 The question of how these domestic actors influence the design of foreign policy, if at all, cannot be explored here but should certainly be addressed in any future research on Fox's foreign policy.

old ones: free trade and globalisation were fairly new by the beginning of the 1990s, but not democracy and human rights. What was new in Zedillo's policy, and even more so in Fox's, is the way in which these issues were addressed.[102] As methods are concerned, it would be difficult to determine how 'more new' were Salinas's from those used by Echeverría or López Portillo, for example. In brief, being such a relative notion, a *new* foreign policy should be seen more than anything as a rhetorical resource used by two governments to distance themselves from the previous government.

How *active* is *active*? Mexican governments have been 'active' in the sense of 'doing something' (although perhaps not taking the initiative) since the end of the Second World War: with the United States, in the UN and the OAS, and other multilateral fora. NAFTA may be seen as a sort of 'grand-strategy', different from previous initiatives in the amount of energy, effort, and resources it absorbed. Comparable enterprises may be Echeverría's Charter of Economic Rights and Duties and López Portillo's policy to Central America, and even de la Madrid's efforts in Contadora: they did involve a lot of activity and resources from Mexican diplomacy but, unlike NAFTA they were not entirely successful. Salinas's commercial diplomacy achieved what it was supposed to achieve, i.e., the Treaty, whatever the costs and consequences in the medium and long term. It remains to be seen whether Fox's active policy continues until the end of his term, presumably to contribute to the consolidation of political change in Mexico. The question, however, should be how effective has foreign policy been, and not how *active* or *new*. This is, of course, a subject for another paper.

How different can Mexican foreign policy become over time? It obviously depends on the objectives, interests and resources, domestic and international, of Mexican governments. So far, Mexican foreign policy has been defensive and 'progressive', has advanced the cause of the Third

---

102 As quoted by Federico Salas, Castañeda pointed out before the Senate that the topic of human rights was not new at all as it was contemplated in the Mexican Constitution. Furthermore, Mexico had reiterated its government's commitments to human rights by signing the UN Charter. Federico Salas, 'Democracia y derechos humanos como política exterior,' in Rafael Fernández de Castro (ed.), *Cambio y continuidad en la política exterior de México. México en el mundo 2002* (Mexico: Ariel-ITAM-AMC, 2002), p. 167.

World and the South, supported revolution and change in Central America, embraced economic neo-liberalism, and has more recently taken on the banner of democracy and human rights. It has reacted to events and it has taken the initiative; it has been mostly 'diplomatic' and it has committed material resources. What may the scope of action of Mexican foreign policy be?

Beginning with *the outside*, the United States is – and will continue to be – a key point of reference, and as González reminds us, power asymmetry between the two countries has not significantly diminished, despite Mexico's open economy and NAFTA. Mexico's economic and geopolitical importance for the United States has certainly increased, but so has Mexican dependence on the United States.[103] However, the heart of the matter is, and has always been, how such dependence influences Mexican foreign policy. As a reaction to a powerful neighbour, Mexican governments' pursued an autonomous foreign policy as a means of stressing their own independence – at least publicly. And the 'agreement to disagree' was a useful arrangement: Mexico did have room for manoeuvre even at the height of the Cold War. The question that follows is how unipolarity and NAFTA are modifying this situation, and the answer has two parts to it: in terms of Mexico–US relations as such, and Mexico's positions regarding other issues in international politics. As the paper demonstrated, there has been a clear tendency towards bilateralism in Mexico's international relations over the last twenty years, although efforts have been made to 'balance' and 'diversify' them, either by signing trade agreements with many countries and regions, or by participating in multilateral initiatives in the UN and in the OAS, or in *ad hoc* diplomacy. On the other hand, the Mexican governments have retained their capacity to dissent from the United States, the war in Iraq being the most recent example. Such capacity, however, is determined by various factors, such as the sort of events taking place in world politics and in this sense, Mexico's margin of action is still defined by the parameters implicit in the

---

103 According to González, the US economy is around twenty-five times larger than Mexico's, and the per capita income gap ratio between the two countries is still one to eight. In brief, Mexico's dependence on the United States is now greater than ever. 'Foreign Policy Strategies,' p. 159.

'agreement to disagree'. A second important element defining Mexico's standings regarding international affairs – dissenting or not with the United States – is of course *the inside*. If Mexico's domestic change means a plurality of views and values that influence foreign policy, could a Mexican government acknowledge that its interests may coincide with those of its northern neighbour for reasons that have nothing to do with bilateral relations or Mexico's economic dependence on the United States?

In effect, if Mexico consolidates internal change in a democratic direction, a more active Congress or public opinion may have greater influence in the definition of foreign policy. Additionally, if *alternancia* becomes a practice in Mexican politics, the contents of foreign policy may change. It would be interesting to see what the foreign policy of a PRD government would be: would it project democratic values, or a leftist agenda? The so-called Mexican transition would therefore constitute a valuable case to test the 'regime type' approaches in a framework of international change, but with one constant variable: the overwhelming presence of the United States.

www.ingramcontent.com/pod-product-compliance
Ingram Content Group UK Ltd.
Pitfield, Milton Keynes, MK11 3LW, UK
UKHW040610160426
5217IPUK00033B/238